The Contention of Ajax and Ulysses for the Armor of Achilles by James Shirley

As It was nobly represented by young Gentlemen of quality, at a private Entertainment of some persons of Honour.

James Shirley was born in London in September 1596.

His education was through a collection of England's finest establishments: Merchant Taylors' School, London, St John's College, Oxford, and St Catharine's College, Cambridge, where he took his B.A. degree in approximately 1618.

He first published in 1618, a poem entitled Echo, or the Unfortunate Lovers.

As with many artists of this period full details of his life and career are not recorded. Sources say that after graduating he became "a minister of God's word in or near St Albans." A conversion to the Catholic faith enabled him to become master of St Albans School from 1623–25.

He wrote his first play, Love Tricks, or the School of Complement, which was licensed on February 10th, 1625. From the given date it would seem he wrote this whilst at St Albans but, after its production, he moved to London and to live in Gray's Inn.

For the next two decades, he would write prolifically and with great quality, across a spectrum of thirty plays; through tragedies and comedies to tragicomedies as well as several books of poetry. Unfortunately, his talents were left to wither when Parliament passed the Puritan edict in 1642, forbidding all stage plays and closing the theatres.

Most of his early plays were performed by Queen Henrietta's Men, the acting company for which Shirley was engaged as house dramatist.

Shirley's sympathies lay with the King in battles with Parliament and he received marks of special favor from the Queen.

He made a bitter attack on William Prynne, who had attacked the stage in Histriomastix, and, when in 1634 a special masque was presented at Whitehall by the gentlemen of the Inns of Court as a practical reply to Prynne, Shirley wrote the text—The Triumph of Peace.

Shirley spent the years 1636 to 1640 in Ireland, under the patronage of the Earl of Kildare. Several of his plays were produced by his friend John Ogilby in Dublin in the first ever constructed Irish theatre; The Werburgh Street Theatre. During his years in Dublin he wrote The Doubtful Heir, The Royal Master, The Constant Maid, and St. Patrick for Ireland.

In his absence from London, Queen Henrietta's Men sold off a dozen of his plays to the stationers, who naturally, enough published them. When Shirley returned to London in 1640, he finished with the Queen Henrietta's company and his final plays in London were acted by the King's Men.

On the outbreak of the English Civil War Shirley served with the Earl of Newcastle. However when the King's fortunes began to decline he returned to London. There his friend Thomas Stanley gave him help and thereafter Shirley supported himself in the main by teaching and publishing some educational works under the Commonwealth. In addition to these he published during the period of dramatic eclipse four small volumes of poems and plays, in 1646, 1653, 1655, and 1659.

It is said that he was "a drudge" for John Ogilby in his translations of Homer's Iliad and the Odyssey, and survived into the reign of Charles II, but, though some of his comedies were revived, his days as a playwright were over.

His death, at age seventy, along with that of his wife, in 1666, is described as one of fright and exposure due to the Great Fire of London which had raged through parts of London from September 2nd to the 5th.

He was buried at St Giles in the Fields, in London, on October 29th, 1666.

Index of Contents

THE SPEAKERS
Ajax Telamon.
Ulysses.
Agamemnon.
Diomedes.
Menelaus.
Nestor.
Calchas.
Thersander.
Polybrontes, a small Souldier.
Lysippus   } Pages.
Didimus   }
Souldiers.
Attendants.

SCENE

The Grecian Camp

SCENE I

Near the Tent of Agamemnon

DIDIMUS, ULYSSES, his Page, **LYSIPPUS, AJAX** his **PAGE**.

DIDIMUS
Why how now Insolence?

[**LYSIPPUS** justles **DIDIMUS**.

LYSIPPUS
You know me Sir?

DIDIMUS
For one that wants good manners; yes, I know
Your name, and best relation, you attend
A Page on Ajax Telamon.

LYSIPPUS
And you
In such an office wait upon Ulysses,
But with this difference, that I am your better,
In reference to my Lord, as he exceeds
Your Master both in Fortitude and Honour:
Therefore I take this boldness to instruct
Your diminutive Worship in convenient duties,
And that hereafter when you see me pass,
You may descend, and vail, and know fit distance.

DIDIMUS
To you descend, and vail? to you? poor Rat!
Is he not poison'd, that he swells so strangely:
I would bestow this admonition, that
You talk within your limits, I may finde
A pity for your folly, while you make
Comparisons with me, but let your tongue
Preserve a modestie, and not dare to name
My Lord, without a reverence, and not
In the same week your Master is in mention,
Least I chastise you.

LYSIPPUS
Ha, ha, prodigie!

The Monkey grins, the Pigmie would be Rampant:
Sirrah, 'tis I pronounce, if you have
A minde to lose one of your lugs, or quit
Some teeth that stick impertinent in your gums,
Orrun the hazard of an eye, or have
Your haunches kick'd into a gentle cullice,
Or tell your Master in whose cause you have
Deserv'd a cudgelling, and merited
A crutch to carry home your broken bodie;
Talk on, and when it is too late, you may
Repent your impudence.

DIDIMUS

Mightie man of gingerbread!
Is not your name Lysippus? what mad Dog
Has bit thee; thou art wilde, hast lost thy senses?

LYSIPPUS

You'l finde, I have not.

DIDIMUS

Is all this in earnest?
And hast thou so much ignorance, to think
That lump of flesh, thy Master (a thing meant
By nature for a flail, and bang the sheafs)
Is fit to be in competition
With the wise Prince of Ithaca? whose name
Shines like a Constellation throughout Greece,
And is lookt at with admiration
By friends and enemies? for shame retract
Thy gross opinion, it is possible
Thou maist retrive thy lost wits,

LYSIPPUS

Verie well
Then, you do think my little spawn of Policie,
That your slie Master, the oyl-tongu'd Ulysses,
Will win the prize to day, Achilles Armour;
And that the Kinglie Judges, and grave Counsel
Will give it against Ajax.

DIDIMUS

In true wisdom,
As to the best deserver.

[They fight.

LYSIPPUS

Dandiprat.

CALCHAS
Remove your selves, and pettie differences,
This place is meant the scene for a contention
Between the valiant Ajax Telamon,
And the far fam'd Ulysses, who shall best
Me it to wear the great Achilles Arms:
Methinks I see Heavens mightie windows open,
And those great souls, whom noble actions here
Translated to take place among the Stars:
Look down, and listen with much expectation
Of this daies glorie. The rough winds (least they
Should interrupt the plea of these Competitors)
Stand close committed in their horrid caves,
And habus drest in all his brightest beams,
Curbs in his Steeds to stay, to wait upon
The great Decision.
Silence, no noise prophane this place, and may
The soul of wisdom be at this great Council.

[Exeunt **DIDIMUS** and **LYSIPPUS**.

[Enter **OFFICERS** one after another, bearing the Pieces of Achilles Armour, after them in state,
AGAMEMNON, NESTOR, MENELAUS, DIOMEDES, THERSANDER, &c.

AGAMEMNON
I need not, Grecian Princes, spend much time
Or Language, in discousing the occasion
Why this great Council hath been call'd; Achilles,
Whose very name will be enough to fill
The breath of fame, is here agen concern'd,
Nor can his honour'd ashes be without
Contention in his sacred Urn, until
The difference between these great Competitors
Be reconciled.

CAPTAIN
They both, great Agamemnon, are prepar'd,
And cheerful, as when Honour call'd them forth
To fight, impatient of delay, or danger.

AGAMEMNON
Attend them hither,

DIOMEDES

Let the Officers
Take care the Souldiers press not past their limit.

[Enter before **AJAX**, his **PAGE**, bearing his Target.

[**AJAX** appears, with lightning in his eyes. His big heart seems to boil with rage.

MENELAUS.
He was ever passionate:
Here comes Ulysses.

[Enter **ULYSSES**, with his **PAGE**, as before, he makes obeysance, and sets down in a Chair.

A man of other temper, and as far
From being transported with unhandsome anger,
He seems to smile.

AGAMEMNON
They have both deserv'd
For their great service in this expedition,
We should with calm, and most impartial souls
Hear and determine; therefore, if you please,
Because the hours are precious, I shall
Desire them lose no time.

DIOMEDES
We all submit, and shall obey your prudence.

AGAMEMNON
You honour much:
Your Agamemnon—Princes then to you,
I hope you have brought hither, with your persons,
Nothing but what your honours may consent too;
Speak your selves freely then, these are your Judges
Who are not onely great in birth and titles,
And therefore bring no thoughts to stain their honour,
But bound by obligation of one Countrey,
Will love, and do your name and valours justice.
There lies your great reward, Achilles Arms,
Forg'd by the subtile art of him, that fram'd
Ioves Thunderbolts, pride of Cyclopian labours,
He that is meant by his kinde stars, to have
The happy wearing of them next, may write
Himself a Champion or the Gods, and Heaven,
Against a race of Gyants that world scale it:
I have said, and we with silence now as deep
As that doth wait on midnight, and as fixt
As marble Images, expect your pleasure.

[**AJAX** rises and looks about him.

AJAX
Great Jove, immure my heart, or girt it with
Some ribs of steel, lest it break through this flesh,
And with a flame contracted from just fury,
Set fire on all the world: How am I fallen?
How shrunk to nothing? my fame ravish'd from me?
That this sly talking Prince is made my Rival
In great Achilles Armour: Is it day?
And can a Cloud darker than night, so muffle
Your eyes, they cannot reach the Promontory,
Beneath which now the Grecian fleet rides safe,
Which I so late rescued from Trojan flames,
When Hector frightful, like a Globe of fire,
By his example taught the enraged youth
To brandish lightning; but I cannot talk,
Nor knows he how to fight, unless 'ith dark
With shadows. I confess, his eloquence
And tongue are mighty, but Pelides sword
And armour were not made things to be talk'd on,
But worn and us'd, and when you shall determine
My juster claim, it will be fame enough
For him, to boast, he strove with Ajax Telamon.
And lost the prize, due onely to my merit.

LYSIPPUS
Now Didimus, how goes Ulysses pulse?
Run to his Tent, and fetch him some strong waters.

DIDIMUS
This storm shakes not a leafe, it had been more
Honour for Ajax Telamon to have hir'd
A Trumpeter, than make this noise himself.

AGAMEMNON
Silence.

[The **DUKE** proceeds.

AJAX
I am asham'd
And blush, that I can plead so vast a marit:
Why am I not less honourable? a cheaper
Portion of worth, weigh'd in the ballance, with
This Rival, would so croud, and fill my scale,
His vertues, like a thin and trembling vapour,

Would lose themselves i'th ayr, or stick a Comet
Upon Heavens face, from whence the matter spent,
It would fall down, the sport and scorn of Children,
Allow me then less valiant, pinch all
The Laurels from my brow, that else would grow there,
The honour of my birth and blood must lift me
Above the Competition with Ulysses;
My Father was Duke Telamon, a name
Fatal to Troy, companion to Alcides,
Whom in the expedition to Colchos,
Argo was proud to bear: his father Aeacus,
Who for his exemplary justice here,
Was by Eternal Patent from the Gods,
Made Judge of souls; him Iupiter begot
On fair Egina, from whose womb, I write
My self a third from Iove: But let not this
Entitle me to great Achilles arms,
Without my interest in his blood: Our fathers
Grew from one royal stem, I am his Kinsman,
And I demand in this, but just inheritance.
In what relation of blood can then
Ulysses. of a strange and forfeit race,
Equal in fraud to his Progenitor,
Condemn'd to labour at the restless stone,
Lay claim to Achilles Arms?

CALCHAS
What, asleep Thersander?

THERSANDER
No, no, I observe every word, Ulysses has
Said very well, he was ever a good Orator.

CALCHAS
You are mistaken, Sir, 'tis Ajax pleads,
Ulysses has not spoke one word.

THERSANDER
Wast Ajax?
I cry you mercy, it was very handsome,
And to the purpose in my opinion,
Who ever said it.

AGAMEMNON
I intreat your silence.

THERSANDER
With all my heart.

AJAX

It is wonder Princes,
That this Dulichyan King dare bring his face
Before a Sun-beam, and expose that brand
Of infamie, the name of Coward, writ
In Leprous Characters upon his brow,
To the worlds eye.

ULYSSES

How Telamon?

AJAX

Ulysses,
'Tis I, that said it, and these Kings may all
Remember, when most wretchedly, to save
Those tender limbs of yours, and that warp'd face,
When Greece rise up, one man to punish Troy,
Thou cowardly didst counterfeit a madness,
Till Palamedes pull'd that vizor off.
Was Ajax Telamon at that sordid posture?
Nay, was not I the first in field, and eager
To engage my person in these Wars of Troy?
(Witness thou sacred Genius of our Countrey)
As a curl'd youth could fly to meet a Mistris,
And print his fervour on her amorous lip:
But for his valour since, let Nestor speak;
That good old man made not his age excuse,
Nor his white hairs, that like a Grove of snow,
Shew'd what a Winter dwelt upon his head,
But flung himself on War, when in the heat
Of Battle, over-charg'd with multitudes,
And his horse wounded, he espi'd Ulysses,
To whom in this distress, he call'd for succour,
When he (unworthy of his name and honours)
Left the old man to struggle with his dangers,
To whom the Gods sent ayd. But here's the justice,
He that dishonourably forsook his friend,
Met with an enemy, that made him call
As loud for his relief; I heard that clamour,
And with my sword cut out my passage to thee,
When thou wert quaking at the enemies feet,
And ready to exhale thy panting soul,
I interposed, bestrid thy coward body,
And took thy many deaths upon my Target:
I Ajax brought thee off (my least of honours)
And saved thy wretched life.

DIOMEDES

This Ajax did,
But being done, the honour's over paid,
When he that did the act is Commentator.

AJAX

If thou couldst call again that time Ulysses,
The wounds upon thee, and thy fears of death,
When thou didst skulk behinde my shield, and tremble
At every lightning of a sword, thy soul
Would have a less ambition to contest
For great Pelides Arms.

MENELAUS

Ajax will carry it.

AGAMEMNON

It will
Become our prudence to expect, what may
Be said in answer to this accusation;
I have heard an Orator, with that subtile method
Of art and language, state his Clients cause,
And with such captivating arguments
Prevail'd on every ear, it was concluded,
All law must be in favour of that interest,
But when the adverse part was heard, that which
Appear'd so sacred in the first relation,
Vanish'd, and 'twas the wonder of all men,
By what strange magick they were so deceiv'd:
I speak not this in prejudice of him
That pleads, whom we all know a man made up
Of every masculine vertue, but to stay
(Where two of so much honor are concern'd)
Precipitate, and partial votes of merit:
Ajax Has more to say.

AJAX

I know not how, with safety of mine own,
I should direct your judgements to consider,
That after all this story of my self,
I do not seek these arms, nor court the glory
To wear em, for 'tis justice to pronounce
They seek me, Ajax, and should prompt you to
Believe, I onely worthily can wear 'em.
What hath Ulysses done, he should be nam'd
With Telamon; we have his Chronicle,
He surpriz'd Rhesus in his Tent, a great
And goodly act, nay, had the heart to kill him;

He snatch'd a spy up, Dolon, and dispatcht him
To the other world, a most heroick service!
And had the confidence to filch from Troy,
The dead Palladium, memorable actions:
Fought he with Hector? did he stand immov'd
As I, when I receiv'd upon my cask,
A mighty Javelin that he darted at me?
When you, pale with the wonder of my strength,
Forsook your prayers, and gave me from the Gods
Into my own protection, and at last
I was not overcome, but in the face
Of both the Armies, sent this mighty Champion
Staggering home to Troy.

NESTOR
'Twas a fierce battel,
And Aax lost no honour.

AJAX
Had I done
But this alone, it might be argument
To prefer Ajax Telamon before
Ulysses to that armour; which I'm thinking
How he'll become, or how he dare sustain 'em,
Their very weight will crack his chine, that Burgonet
Will bring his neck in danger of a cramp,
In pitty of his fears, discharge his hope
Of so much steel, he has the art of running,
'Twill much reta d his motion: Are you yet
Considering as doubtful to distinguish us?
Some God convey those arms up on the wings
Of a swift wind into the enemies camp,
Guard'em with all the strength and soul of Troy,
Let every sword mount death upon the point,
And leave us to our single fate, who soonest
Should fetch 'em off: Then you should tell your selves,
How much this Carpet Prince came short of Ajax,
I had rather fight than talk: Now here him tattle.

SOULDIERS [within]
An Ajax, an Ajax

ULYSSES
If my prayers, with your own, renowned Kings,
Could have prevail'd with Heaven, there had been no
Contention for these arms, he might have liv'd
To have enjoy'd them still, and we Achilles.
But since by the unkindeness of our fate,

We are decreed to want him (pardon me
If at that word, unmanly tears break forth)
Who can with greater merit claim the armour,
Than he whose piety to Greece and you,
Engag'd alone his valour to these Wars,
And made him yours. Nor let it be a sin
Ere I proceed, to pray this justice from you,
That since my adversary hath been pleas'd
To make a vertue my reproach, and stain
The name of Eloquence, which in me, is not worth
Your envy, or his rage (since he declares
His incapacity for more than fighting)
You will not judge his dulness an advantage,
Or that which he calls eloquence in me,
A blemish to my cause, who have employ'd
All that the Gods made mine, to serve my Countrey.

DIOMEDES
Thersander,
Are you not asham'd to sleep?

THERSANDER
Ha! no, I sleep?
I have not scap'd a syllable by my honour,
I thought not Ajax half so good an Orator.

DIOMEDES
Ajax? it was Ulysses that spoke last.

THERSANDER
Ulysses? I, I meant Ulysses; did I say Ajax?
Between you and I be it spoken Diomedes,
Ajax is a blockhead.

DIOMEDES
Yet he spoke to purpose.

THERSANDER
I grant you that; nay, nay, let him alone.

AGAMEMNON
Silence.

ULYSSES
The lustre of our birth by Ajax boasted,
Which we derive not from our act or vertue,
We vainly call our own, nature contributes
A common gloss to all our blood, the honours

And swelling titles, pinn'd upon our name,
Chance often stamps upon a Fool or Coward:
But if provok'd by Ajax, I must yield
Him magnified by blood; that title which
He takes from Iove, makes me his Grandchilde too,
Lacrtes was my father; his Arcesius,
Whom Iupiter begot, no difference here,
But that our Family contain'd no Uncle
Banish'd for murther, as in Telamons.
Besides, my mother but remembred, makes
My derivation on both sides Divine,
Which lifts me above Ajax, if I were
No King of Ithaca: but he hath pleaded
A neerer priviledge by being Kinsman,
And calls these arms his just inheritance,
Your wisdom could not chuse but smile to hear him,
Pyrrhus his son is yet alive, and Peleus,
Achilles father, Teucer his next Cousin;
And Ajax to be heir, is worth your wonder;
But you know how to wave impertinence
Of blood or kindred in this cause, nor shall
I need to pray your justice, that we both
May onely charge the ballance with our merits.

DIOMEDES
This is not ranting, he is Master of A worthy temper.

AGAMEMNON
Give him your permissions.

ULYSSES
Ajax hath read, not without mighty lungs,
His own bold Historie, when I shall tell
But my first act for Troy, if it be less
Than all that Ajax yet hath done, or boasted,
And with his own consent too, I quit all:
I have rais'd your expectations up to wonder,
And there I'll fix it, when I name Achilles,
Whose actions for your service, scorning all
Equality, are owing to Ulysses;
And I may call them mine, that made him yours,
By his sword fell the great Priamides
Hoctor, whose single arm carried the strength
And fate of Ilium: The death alone
Of Hector, is an act, if well consider'd,
Doth easily exceed, what hath been done
In all your Grecian Commentaries: I arm'd
Achilles first to do these mighty things,

And for those may deserve Achilles armour,

DIOMEDES
We must acknowledge all the benefits
Of great Achilles valour are a debt
We owe to Ulysses, who discovered him
Under a Female habit, 'twas Ulysses
That made him man again, and our great Champion.

MENELAUS
All this is granted, yet I think Ulysses
Lost little blood in any of these services;
What do you think Thersander?

THERSANDER
I think as the General thinks, he's wise enough.

ULYSSES
But give me leave to offer to your memory
Another service, and reduce your thoughts
To Aulis, when our Army ship'd, and big
With our desires for Troy, for want of wind
Were lock'd in the Eubean Bay at Anchor.
When the Oracle consulted, gave no hope
Of the least breath of Heaven, or gentle gale
To be expected, till Diana's anger
Were first appeas'd by Iphigenias blood;
I melt with the remembrance, and I could
Accuse my faith, but that the publique interest
And all your honours, arm'd me to perswade
Nature, against the stream of her own happiness,
There stands the tear—drown'd father Agamemnon,
Ask his vex'd soul (and let me beg his pardon)
How I did work upon his murmuring heart,
Divided 'twixt a Father and his Countrey,
To give his childe up to the bleeding altar?
Whose drops (too precious to enrich the earth,
The Goddess hid within a cloud) drank up,
And snatcht her soul; whose brighter substance made
One of the fairest Stars that deck yon Canopie.
Had Ajax been employed to have wrought Atrides
When he was angry with the Gods, to have given
His onely pledge, his loved Iphigenia
Up to the Fatal knife, our Grecian fleet,
Had by this time been rotten in the Bay,
And we by a dishonourable return,
Been wounded in our fames to after ages.

AGAMEMNON

This truth is urg'd too home.

ULYSSES

The Deity appeas'd with Virgin Sacrifice,
The winds put on fresh wings, and we arriv'd
Swift as our wishes to affrighted Troy;
Where, after their first battel, they no more
Drew forth their Army, which engag'd us to
Nine horrid Winters expectation:
It would be tedious to relate, how active
My counsels were, during this nine years siege,
When Ajax (onely good at knocks and wrestling)
Was of no use, the bold designs I carried,
My care of our defences and approaches,
Encouraging the Souldier, wearied
And worn away with empty expectations,
How I did apt provisions, arms, and hearts
To fight withal, I shall not here inforce,
When you whose just commands I still obey'd,
Are conscious of my pious undertakings.

AJAX

He'l talk eternally.

ULYSSES

These actions have deserv'd no brand of Coward,
How it may stain his forehead that accus'd me,
Judge you, by the short following story, Princes
There was a time, when Agamemnon was
Deluded by a dream, and bid to leave
The siege, which coming to the Souldiers ear,
(Whose fears were helpt by superstition)
How did they run to'th ships from every quarter:
Where was the torrent of great Ajax valour
So talk'd of, that did bear all things before it?
Why, it was here, that torrent carried him too:
I saw and blush'd at Ajax preparation
To be aboard, (I will not call it running)
How did I, careless of all danger, throw
My self among the Mutineers, and court
The Fugitives to face about agen,
And build themselves a name, and wealth in Troy,
Given over by the Gods to be their captive?
What acted Telamon, but unworthy fears,
And rather coward them by his retreat,
Than teach them honour by his own example.

AJAX

Can Iove hear this? ha!

AGAMEMNON

Look to Ajax.

NESTOR

Contain yourself.

AJAX

Let me fight him here,
Or you are all confederates in my infamy.

NESTOR

For my sake.

AJAX

I am patient—

ULYSSES

Nor am I without wounds, and crimson characters,
Which as her ornament, my bosom carries,
Greater than Telamon can boast, although
He fought with Hector, which was but his Fortune,
And might have been the lot of Agamemnon,
Of Menelaus, Diomed, my self,
And others, who had equally engag'd,
And onely chance preferr'd him to the combate:
But let me not be thought to take from Ajax
His just reward of fortitude, I grant
He did repress the fury of the Trojans,
When they came arm'd in fires against our Navy,
But 'twas nor single valour, that repulst
The numerous enemy. Patroclus had
The armour of Achilles on that day,
Which struck a terrour in the Phrygian courages,
And many Princes swords contributed,
Mine was not idle, and I merit some
Proportion of fame for that days victory;
But if it come with murmuring, defer it,
And make it up in your accounts of honour
Due, for the great Palladium, which I fetch'd
(Assisted by the valiant Diomedes)
Out of the heart of Troy, spight of the Groves
Of Spears, that grew a bright defence about it,
And Swords, whose every motion darted lightning
To guard the fatal Image; in this act
I gave you Troy, till this was ravish'd from 'em,

It was not in your fate to make a conquest,
Ajax and all the Army might have fought
Against the Moon, with as much hope of Victory.

DIOMEDES
This must be granted him a signal Service,
I can attest the danger of this action.

ULYSSES
I blush, I am compell'd to mention these,
But where my honour is traduc'd, 'tis just
To make my fairest vindication:
The wealth of Greece should not have brib'd me to
This Contestation; but Achilles armour
Would strike ambitious thoughts into a Hermite,
Nor will my limbes much tremble to sustain 'em
I had the honour at his death, to carry
His body with all that weight of arms upon it,
And plac'd him in his Tent, although I want
Some bulk of Ajax, I can walk, and fight,
And tell him where he fails, and mark him out
A truer path to Glory, than his strength
Is able to persue, with no more brains
To guide him, than his empty pannier carries:
Wisemen joyn policy with force, the Lyon
Thus with the Fox, makes up the Souldiers emblem.
And now I look on Ajax Telamon,
I may compare him to some specious building,
His body holds vast rooms of entertainment,
And lower parts maintain the Offices,
Onely the Garret, his exalted head,
Useless for wise receipt, is fill'd with lumber,
A Mastiff dares attempt to combate Lyons,
And I'll finde men among your Mercenaries
Shall fly on Hydra's, if you name that valour:
But he, that we call valiant indeed,
Knows how, and when to fight, as well as bleed.

[A great shout within.

SOULDIERS [shouting within]
Ulysses, Ulysses.

AGAMEMNON
Please you withdraw your persons for some minutes,

AJAX
Is't come to this.

ULYSSES
I obey.

AJAX
I scorn to court
Such staggering opinions, and repent
That I once thought you fit to be my Judges.

[Exit

THERSANDER
For my part, with pardon of the Generall,
My voyce shall be to please them both.

AGAMEMNON
Impossible.

THERSANDER
Divide the armour, and compose the difference;
Or give Ulysses, 'cause he has the better
Head-piece, Achilles Helmet; and to Ajax,
Those parts that guard the body.

DIOMEDES
I am for
Ulysses.

NESTOR
He shall have my vote.

MENELAUS
And mine.

AGAMEMNON
Your judgements meet with Agamemnons,
Intreat the Prince of Ithaca return.

[Enter **ULYSSES**.

AGAMEMNON
Sir I congratulate your fate, you have
With the concurrence of our votes, deserv'd
To be the second owner of these arms;
Which as the first reward of all your service,
I in their names present: Nor are these Trophies
More than an earnest, and a glimpse, of those
Eternal Monuments shall Crown your Wisdom;

Where's Ajax Telomon?

OFFICER
Transported hence with fury.

ULYSSES
You have honour'd your Ulysses, and I now
Must call these things my blessing, and your bounty.

AGAMEMNON
Bear them in Triumph to his Tent, and say,
Wisdom, not down-right Valour wins the day;
Better is wise Ulysses in the field,
Than the great Master of the seven-sold Shield.

[Exeunt.

SCENE II

Near the tent of Ajax.

DIDIMUS, LYSIPPUS.

DIDIMUS
I think Lysippus, we may now be friends,
For though you had a minde to quarrel when
The victory was doubtful, I am not
The more exalted for my Masters triumph,
His wit is none of mine; I honour Ajax
In his own arms; for I have seen him do
Brave things.

LYSIPPUS
Thy hand, I love thee Didimus,
And I will love Ulysses for thy sake too.

DIDIMUS
But how does thy Lord Ajax take the business?

LYSIPPUS
He's mad, and rails at heaven and earth, I dare not
Come neer him—Whose this, Polybrontes?

[Enter **POLYBRONTES**

Let us forget all differences, and make

Some sport with him—Polybrontes,
I am proud to see your military face.

DIDIMUS
My Magazine of Valour, I do honour you,
From that exalted trust upon your Skonce,
To the cold iron Star upon your heel, how is't?

LYSIPPUS
How is't my Low, and Mighty Polybrontes?

POLYBRONTES
Tir'd out with killing of the Creature,
Wilde Beasts, and Men, will come into my way;
Some, I look dead, others I take the pains
To cut or quarter, as they move my fury,
The hate of Iuno is entail'd upon
Our generation I think.

DIDIMUS
How, Juno? I pray what kin are you to Hercules?

POLYBRONTES
I am his son, son to the Theban Hercules
That did the mighty Labours; we number twelve,
I have been told too, I am very like him;
There were fifty of us in one night begotten.

DIDIMUS
You are not, Sir, so big bon'd as Hercules altogether.

POLYBRONTES
Hang bones, and flesh, and blood,
It is the soul that's tall, a Gyants spirit.

LYSIPPUS
Not in that body,
A soul can hardly stand upright in't.

POLYBRONTES
'Tis the more dangerous, being confin'd, and must
Break out like lightning.

DIDIMUS
What's that upon your hat?

POLYBRONTES
My case of Tooth-picks.

LYSIPPUS
How, 'tis a Lyons paw.

POLYBRONTES
A Legacy my father left me, part
Of that Nemean Lyon, that he kill'd,
Whose skin he us'd to wear, which since these Wars
I turn'd into a Knapsack, and it carries
A charm against all venemous Beasts, come near it,

DIDIMUS
Vermine he means:
What kinde of belt is this?

POLYBRONTES
This was a Serpent, which at Aulis was
Obsessed to climbe up to the Sparrows nest,
Where having swallowed nine, Calchas presag'd,
We should be nine years at the siege of Troy,
And in the tenth be Conqueros, this I kill'd
With a Flint stone, as it came hissing toward me,
It had ten row of iron teeth.

DIDIMUS
Where are they?

POLYBRONTES
All beaten out with that stone I threw at her.

DIDIMUS
Nothing scapes you then:
But good Sir favour us, to let us know
How many men have fallen by your sword
During our siege, I know you keep a Catalogue.

POLYBRONTES
Not of all,
I onely register within my Diary,
The men of honour that I kill, the rest
I leave to the common bills of Mortality.

LYSIPPUS
The men of honour, I pray, Sir.

POLYBRONTES
They rise to—
·oo in my roll.

DIDIMUS
With your own hand?

POLYBRONTES
Ten Princes, beside two of Priams sons,
Paris and Hector,

LYSIPPUS
Paris is alive.

POLYBRONTES
Not that Paris I kill'd upon my honour.

DIDIMUS
And all the Army knowes, Achilles with
His Mirmidons slew Hector.

POLYBRONTES
From me tell Achilles
'Tis false.

LYSIPPUS
He's dead too.

POLYBRONTES
'Tis well he is so, he that steals my fame,
Must not be long i'th number of the living.

DIDIMUS
You are
The little wonder of the world, you had
Done your self right, to have put in with Ulysses
And Ajax, for the armour.

LYSIPPUS
Had he stood,
There had been no Competitor, Ulysses
Had this day mist his triumph.

POLYBRONTES
Had Ulysses
The armour then?

[Enter **AJAX**.

LYSIPPUS
Given by all Judges.

POLYBRONTES
I believe
The man is so modest, he at mention
Of me, would have recanted his ambition;
Do not I know Ulysses? yes, and Ajax.

AJAX
Ha!

POLYBRONTES
And all the swelling flies that blow the Army,
I'll tell that Ajax, when I see him next,
That I dare fight?

AJAX
With whom Sir, dare you fight?

POLYBRONTES
With any man that shall affront you, Sir,
Renowned Ajax, my soul falls to crums
That day, I do not honour your remembrance.
Ulysses is a Juggler, I do wonder
At's impudence, to stand in competition
With him, that is the man of men, brave Telamon:
Shall I carry him a challenge; prethee let me,
I long to thunder him.

AJAX
Stay Wesel!

POLYBRONTES
Or to Agamemnon, or the best of them,
Would I were in my knapsack nibbling cheese now.

AJAX
I say the word, be dead.

[**AJAX** strikes him.

POLYBRONTES
My brains, my brains!
Ah my own sweet brains; who wants any brains?

AJAX
Art thou not dead?

POLYBRONTES

Oh yes Sir, I am dead,
Give my Ghost leave to walk a little.

AJAX
Come back, your name?

POLYBRONTES
Ah, when I was alive, the Souldiers call'd me—

AJAX
Agamemnon.

POLYBRONTES
I shall be brain'd in earnest!

AJAX
When thou hast past the Stygian Lake, commend me
To Eacus, one of the Infernal Judges.

POLYBRONTES
I will Sir, I am acquainted with his Clark.

AJAX
And when I have made my revenge perfect,
I'll visit him my self.

POLYBRONTES
I'll bring you an answer too.

AJAX
Do so.

POLYBRONTES
I were best to make haste, Sir, Charon stays for me,
And I shall lose my tide.

AJAX
Then vanish.

POLYBRONTES
Presto.

[Exit.

AJAX
There's one dispatch'd, he's company for Ghosts,
I know whose fate is next, and then I leap
To immortality: what cloud is that

Descends so big with prodigy, my steel
Shall give the Monster birth, ha' 'tis Ulysses,
Come to affront me in Achilles armour:

[Enter **CALCHAS**

A thousand serpents creep within my skull:
I'll finde the Cowards soul through all this darkness,
Have at thee Polititian, dost thou bleed?
Now I have met we'e, thanks to my good sword,
I kiss thy cold lips, for this brave revenge,
Thou art my own, without competitor,
And must be my last refuge and companion.

CALCHAS
Alas poor Telamon!

AJAX
Who calls Telamon?

CALCHAS
One you have known and lov'd; can you forget
Calchas so soon?

AJAX
Our Grecian Prophet, you are very welcome,
What news from the upper World? do they agree
In heaven? we are all to pieces.

CALCHAS
I am trusted
With a direction to you, the sacred powers
You serve—

AJAX
Speak on, but let me tell you as a friend,
They have not us'd me kindely, but no matter,
I'll be my own revenger.

CALCHAS
Sir, take heed.
How you provoke their anger, or contemn
Their Precepts, for the partial acts of men,
They know, and pitty that a man so valiant,
Should for a trifle lose his manly temper:
You are not, Sir, forgotten by the Gods
And I am sent, their Prophet to acquaint you,
That what you lost alive by humane Judges,

Their divine Justice shall restore with honour
To your calm dust; for know, those very arms
In which Ulysses triumphs now, shall be
Snatcht from him by a tempest, and shall land
A floating treasure upon Ajax Tomb,
And by their stay convince the future age,
Who best deserv'd e'm; be not then unman'd,
And thus deface the beauties of your reason.

AJAX
I thank 'em, they are pleas'd, when I am dead
To make a restitution to my fame,
And send me home the armour, this is something,
I'll make my self in a capacity
By death to be an object of their justice,
I'll dye immediately, I can do't my self.

CALCHAS
Your Piety avert so black a deed!
This is a way to make the world suspect
The worth of all your former actions,
And that they were not births Legitimate,
Born from true honour, but the spurious issue
Of an unguided heat, or chance: How shall
We think, that man is truly valiant,
And fit to be engag'd in things of fright
And danger, that wants courage to sustain
An injury? it shews a fear of others,
To be reveng'd upon our selves, and he
Is not so much a Coward that flies death,
As he that suffers, and doth fear to live:
Besides, this will enlarge your enemies triumph,
And in the world opinions, be granted
A tame concession to his worth; nay men,
And with much face of reason, may affirm,
Ulysses did not onely win the arms,

AJAX
Therefore I will dye
With my own hand, and save that infamy;
I am resolved, all fate shall not prevent it:
Leave me:

CALCHAS
I must not.

AJAX
I am not confin'd

To place, thy office yet is thy protection,
Do not presume to follow, left my rage
Make me forget your person, and by sad
Mistake, I turn the Priest into a Sacrifice:
Go tell the world I am dead, and make it known,
That Ajax fell by no hand but his own.

[Exit.

CALCHAS
This will turn all our Triumph into mourning,

[Exeunt.

SCENE III

Another part of the Camp.

[**CALCHAS** before the body of **AJAX**, supported by six Princes, **AGAMEMNON, DIOMEDES, MENELAUS, THERSANDER, NESTOR, ULYSSES**, following the Hearse, as going to the Temple.

CALCHAS
The glories of our blood and state,
are shadows, not substantial things,
There is no armour against fate,
Death lays his icy hand on Kings,
Scepter and Crown,
Must tumble down,
And in the dust be equal made,
With the poor crooked sithe and spade,
Some men with swords may reap the field,
and plant fresh laurels where they kill,
But their strong nerves at last must yield,
They tame but one another still;
Early or late,
They stoop to fate,
And must give up their murmuring hreath,
When they pale Captives creep to death.
The Garlands wither on your brow,
Then boast no more your mighty deeds,
Upon Deaths purple Altar now,
See where the Victor-victim bleeds,
Your beads must come,
To the cold Tomb,
Onely the actions of the just
Smell sweet, and blossom in their dust.

[This was afterwards sung in parts, the Musick excellently composed by Mr. Ed. Coleman.]

AGAMEMNON
Set forward to the Temple, this was once
A day of Triumph, but the death of Ajax
Will make it dark within our Calendar;
Joys are obortive, or not born to last,
And our bright days are quickly overcast.

[Exeunt.

JAMES SHIRLEY – A CONCISE BIBLIOGRAPHY

The following includes years of first publication, and of performance if known, together with dates of licensing by the Master of the Revels if available.

TRAGEDIES
The Maid's Revenge (licensed 9th February 1626; printed, 1639)
The Traitor (licensed 4th May 1631; printed, 1635)
Love's Cruelty (licensed 14th November 1631; printed, 1640)
The Politician (acted, 1639; printed, 1655)
The Cardinal (licensed 25th May 1641; printed, 1652).

TRAGI-COMEDIES
The Grateful Servant (licensed 3rd November 1629 as The Faithful Servant; printed 1630)
The Young Admiral (licensed 3rd July 1633; printed 1637)
The Coronation (licensed 6th February 1635, as Shirley's, but printed in 1640 as a work of John Fletcher)
The Duke's Mistress (licensed 18th January 1636; printed 1638)
The Gentleman of Venice (licensed 30th October 1639; printed 1655)
The Doubtful Heir (printed 1652), licensed as Rosania, or Love's Victory in 1640
The Imposture (licensed 10th November 1640; printed 1652)
The Court Secret (printed 1653).

COMEDIES
Love Tricks, or the School of Complement (licensed 10th February 1625; printed under its subtitle, 1631)
The Wedding (ca. 1626; printed 1629)
The Brothers (licensed 4th November 1626; printed 1652)
The Witty Fair One (licensed 3rd October 1628; printed 1633)
The Humorous Courtier (licensed 17th May 1631; printed 1640).
The Changes, or Love in a Maze (licensed 10th January 1632; printed 1639)
Hyde Park (licensed 20th April 1632; printed 1637)
The Ball (licensed 16th November 1632; printed 1639)
The Bird in a Cage, or The Beauties (licensed 21st January 1633; printed 1633)
The Gamester (licensed 11th November 1633; printed 1637)
The Example (licensed 24th June 1634; printed 1637)

The Opportunity (licensed 29th November 1634; printed 1640)
The Lady of Pleasure (licensed 15th October 1635; printed 1637)
The Royal Master (acted and printed 1638)
The Constant Maid, or Love Will Find Out the Way (printed 1640)
The Sisters (licensed 26th April 1642; printed 1653).
Honoria and Mammon (printed 1659)

DRAMAS

A Contention for Honor and Riches (printed 1633), morality play
The Triumph of Peace (licensed 3rd February 1634; printed 1634), masque
The Arcadia (printed 1640), pastoral tragicomedy
St. Patrick for Ireland (printed 1640), neo-miracle play
The Triumph of Beauty (ca. 1640; printed 1646), masque
The Contention of Ajax and Ulysses (printed 1659), entertainment
Cupid and Death (performed 26th March 1653; printed 1659), masque

www.ingramcontent.com/pod-product-compliance
Lightning Source LLC
Chambersburg PA
CBHW060108050426
42448CB00011B/2652